NATIONS IN CONFLICT

SUDAN

by Chris Hughes

BLACKBIRCH PRESS

An imprint of Thomson Gale, a part of The Thomson Corporation

Detroit • New York • San Francisco • San Diego • New Haven, Conn. • Waterville, Maine • London • Munich

Photo credits:
Cover Image: © Zohra Bensemra/Reuters/CORBIS
AP/Wide World Photos, 27, 30
© Benjamin Lowy/CORBIS, 32
© Bettmann/CORBIS, 15, 18, 24
© Caroline Penn/CORBIS, 20
© Chris Rainier/CORBIS, 23
© Christine Osborne/CORBIS, 13
Getty Images, 6, 7, 34, 35, 36, 39
© Lynsey Addario/CORBIS, 43
© Paul Almasy/CORBIS, 11
© Reuters/CORBIS, 29
© Robert Maass/CORBIS, 8
Steve Zmina, 5
© Wendy Stone/CORBIS, 25
© Zohra Bensemra/Reuters/CORBIS, 41

LIBRARY OF CONGRESS CATALOGING-IN-PUBLICATION DATA

Hughes, Christopher (Christopher A.), 1968–
    Sudan / by Chris Hughes.
        p. cm. — (Nations in conflict)
    Includes bibliographical references and index.
    ISBN 1-4103-0553-8 (hardcover : alk. paper)
    1. Sudan—Juvenile literature. I. Title. II. Series.

    DT154.6.H83 2005
    962.4—dc22

                                    2005009566

Printed in the United States of America
10 9 8 7 6 5 4 3 2 1

CONTENTS

A Land Divided

In June 2004, U.S. secretary of state Colin Powell visited the Darfur region of western Sudan to investigate reports of widespread violence and atrocities. In his report back to the U.S. Senate, he stated: "Genocide has been committed in Darfur and . . . the government of Sudan and the Janjaweed bear responsibility."[1] Genocide is defined by the United Nations (UN) as "acts committed with intent to destroy, in whole or in part, a national, ethnical, racial or religious group."[2] In the case of Darfur, the targeted ethnic groups are black Africans, and those most often accused of the attacks are Arab militia called the janjaweed. In Arabic, *janjaweed* can be translated as "man with a gun on a horse," or "evil horseman." Powell accused the mostly Arab government of Sudan of backing the janjaweed, a claim supported by many outside observers.

By 2005, the crisis in Darfur had already caused more than 70,000 deaths and left more than 2 million people homeless, yet it is only one of a long series of crises that has afflicted Sudan since its independence in 1956. Conflicts over religion, race, territory, politics, and natural resources have turned Sudan into one of the world's most dangerous countries, with

(Above) A Sudanese man surveys the ruined remains of a village destroyed by janjaweed militiamen in September 2004.

(Left) Sudanese refugees fleeing violence in Darfur in 2004 stop to collect water from a makeshift well.

more than 2 million people killed since 1983. In fact, Sudan has enjoyed only eleven years of relative peace since 1956.

Sudan has also been involved in world events that have increased its troubles. Sudan's government has been accused of aiding international terrorists, including Osama bin Laden, responsible for the September 2001 attacks on the United States. It has also been caught up in some of the struggles of its neighbors, whose wars at times have spilled over into Sudan. The UN lists Sudan as one of the 50 least developed countries in the world. Sudan's problems are complex, and many are deeply rooted in the faiths and history of Sudan's people.

CHAPTER ONE

Place, People, Past

Located in northern Africa, Sudan is the continent's largest nation. It borders the Red Sea and shares borders with Egypt, Libya, Chad, Central African Republic, Congo, Uganda, Kenya, Ethiopia, and Eritrea. Northern Sudan is covered by the Libyan and Nubian deserts, which are part of the Sahara desert region. The Nile River runs the length of the nation. South of Khartoum, the capital, the land becomes more tropical and includes more fertile areas, along with one of the world's largest swamps, called the Sudd.

The northern part of Sudan is populated mostly by Arabic-speaking peoples. The majority of northerners are Muslims, meaning they follow the religion of Islam. In the south, most of the people follow the indigenous, or original, religions of their own ethnic group or tribe. About 5 percent of Sudanese are Christian; they also live mostly in the south. In all, Sudan is made up of more than 600 ethnic groups, speaking 400 different languages and dialects. Most of the black Africans in the south are farmers. Many of the northern Arabs, historically, were herders of camel or cattle, moving their animals across the deserts and dry regions in search of water and grazing areas. Over the course of the 20th century, many of the nomadic Arab families settled into towns and cities.

A Sudanese couple travels through the desert of northern Africa.

Early History

In ancient times, northern Sudan was called Nubia. There, a kingdom called Cush interacted with the powerful Egyptian empire to the north. Over time, some elements of Egyptian and Nubian culture blended together.

In 750 B.C., the armies of Cush conquered Egypt. The Cushite king, Piye, declared himself pharaoh, or ruler, of all of Egypt and Nubia. Piye and his family ruled Egypt for 90 years as Egypt's Twenty-fifth Dynasty, until they were defeated by the Assyrian empire from Asia. The Nubian leaders fled Egypt and eventually moved their own capital to the city of Meroë, on the banks of the Nile in southern Nubia. Its location helped it to flourish as a center of trade, and by about 300 B.C., Meroë's kingdom combined elements of Egyptian, Greek, and central African cultures.

Sudan's Religious Mix

The culture of Meroë had disappeared by about A.D. 300, and Nubia was divided into several small kingdoms. In the 6th century, missionaries brought Christianity to Nubia. In the next century, Islam began to spread throughout the Middle East and into northern Africa. Though the Nubian Christians did not convert, relations between Muslims and Christians remained peaceful despite a few conflicts.

Around the 14th century, the Christian kingdoms began to fall, and Muslim rulers, called sultans, took control. In the southern villages, Arab merchants developed a profitable slave trade as early as the 7th century. Some slaves were taken to serve the Arab leaders of the region, others were sold to the Middle East, and over time, many were transported to

With its decoratively painted façade, this building is a traditional structure of Nubia in northern Sudan.

the Americas. Slavery caused many black Africans in southern Sudan to fear and resent the Arabs and to resist Islam, which they associated with the slave trade.

Egyptian Control

In 1821, Egyptian forces conquered the northern region of Sudan, expanding Egypt's control over the southern Nile Valley. At the time, Egypt itself was a part of the Ottoman Empire that stretched from modern-day Turkey and eastern Europe across the Middle East and into northern Africa. Although Egypt claimed possession of all Sudan, disease and transportation difficulties in the swampy Sudd kept them from achieving any true control over the south, and in the west they did not actually conquer the region of Darfur until 1874.

MUHAMMAD AHMAD: THE MAHDI

Muhammad Ahmad ibn as-Sayyid 'Abd Allāh was born into a family of boat builders in northern Sudan in 1844. Muhammad focused his energies on religious studies from an early age, and while he was a teenager he became involved in Sufism. Sufism is a philosophy associated with Islam that encourages its followers to pursue a deep personal relationship with God by observing strict religious practices.

As Muhammad Ahmad grew, his abilities as a speaker developed. By age 27, he was widely recognized as a religious teacher, and he preached in favor of living strictly and simply in accordance with the *Koran*, Islam's holy book. As he taught, he also became aware of growing resentment against British and Egyptian rulers of Sudan. This resentment grew after the arrival of British general Charles Gordon, who threatened to end the profitable slave trade in 1877.

In 1881, Muhammad proclaimed himself Al Mahdi al Muntazar, or "the awaited guide in the right path." The Mahdi declared that he was sent by God to prepare for the second coming of the Prophet Isa (Jesus) before the final judgment. He demanded a purification of Islam, calling on all Muslims to join a jihad, or holy war, against the British and Egyptian forces. His followers were called the Ansar.

From 1882 through 1885, the Ansar won a series of battles against the foreign armies. In January 1885, they captured Khartoum, killing Gordon and delivering his head to the Mahdi's tent. The British and Egyptians withdrew, leaving the Mahdi in command of almost all of Sudan.

His rule, called the Mahdiyah, was a strict one. The Mahdi demanded that all people live according to the strict laws of the *Koran*. He even modified the five pillars, or basic teachings, of the *Koran* to support his government. In addition to the statement of faith required of all Muslims, he added the statement "Muhammad Ahmad is the Mahdi of God and the representative of His Prophet." Instead of the required holy trip to Mecca, the Mahdi encouraged service in his jihad, and instead of the required donations to the poor, he required payment to the state.

The Mahdi died of typhoid fever in June 1885, but his followers continued his jihad. Between 1887 and 1893, Ansar forces attempted to invade Ethiopia, Eritrea, Egypt, and the lands south of Sudan. These attempts were eventually all defeated, and in 1895 the British and Egyptians returned. In 1898, at the Battle of Omdurman, a force of 25,800 men defeated the 52,000-man Ansar army, retaking Sudan and ending the Mahdiyah.

A man prays at the tomb of Muhammad Ahmad, known as the religious leader, the Mahdi, in Omdurman, Sudan.

In 1823, Egyptian leaders established Khartoum as its capital in Sudan and encouraged the trade of slaves and ivory. Eventually, Europeans, who had come to oppose slavery, forced the Egyptians to give up the slave trade, but even as they outlawed it in northern Sudan, it continued to be an important part of the south's economy.

Rise of the Ansar

By 1870, Britain had become more influential in Egypt than the Ottomans, bringing in British soldiers and politicians to run most Egyptian affairs. In 1877, Charles Gordon, a British officer commanding mostly Egyptian troops, made a serious effort to end slavery in Sudan. This attempt sparked a revolt in 1881 led by a Sudanese Arab, Muhammad Ahmad, who called himself the Mahdi, or "the expected one." His followers were called the Ansar ("the followers"). The Mahdi launched his revolt to rid Sudan of the outsiders from Egypt and Britain. In 1885, the Ansar was successful, and Egyptian and British forces withdrew from all of Sudan. The Mahdi extended his power over the region, enforcing strict laws of Islam. When the Mahdi died in 1885, his followers continued their control over the nation.

British Dominance

In 1898, the British and Egyptians returned. A joint Anglo-Egyptian army defeated the Mahdist army at the Battle of Omdurman, and Sudan was declared to be under the condominium, or joint authority, of Britain and Egypt. Under this agreement, Egypt officially appointed the ruler of Sudan, but the British became the real power in the country. They ran

An illustration depicts the British and Egyptian defeat of the Mahdist army at the Battle of Omdurman in 1898.

northern and southern Sudan as two separate regions and limited travel between them. Choosing to spend most of their efforts and finances developing the north, the British hoped to join southern Sudan to territory they already controlled in Kenya and Uganda. Although unsuccessful in their attempt to separate northern and southern Sudan, the British policies widened an ever-increasing gap between the regions.

For the most part, British rule over Sudan was peaceful. In 1922, Britain gave up its political dominance over Egypt. After the British governor-general of Sudan was assassinated in Egypt in 1924, the British moved to take complete control of Sudan, ordering all Egyptian troops and government workers out of Sudan and replacing them with British and Sudanese citizens.

Over the next two decades, the British allowed regional leaders to gain more control over local affairs. In the north, these leaders were almost always Arab Muslims, and the Ansar, who had formed a political party called the Umma, were given many positions of leadership. In the south, where Islam was less common, tribal chiefs were given limited authority.

In 1946, the British announced that the south would join the north under one government. Southern Sudanese resisted; the new government's language would be Arabic, and very few spaces in the government would be reserved for southerners. The stage was set for independence, but it was also set for a clash between north and south.

Independent Sudan

In 1954, Sudan's first parliament was installed as a step toward full independence. The British handed over hundreds of government positions to the Sudanese, but only four to southerners. Facing a government of Arab Muslims from the north, southern leaders felt ignored by the new state. In August 1955, southern soldiers launched a revolt. When Sudan officially became independent on January 1, 1956, a civil war had already begun.

A political party called the National Unionist Party, or NUP, with strong ties to Egypt, led the first government. Its members had to write a constitution, control the uprising in the south, and build foreign relations. The NUP faced political opposition from several parties and was replaced within a few months by an Umma-supported government.

Military Rule

For two years, the government made little progress addressing Sudan's problems. Finally, in 1958, a military general named Ibrahim Abboud led a coup, or takeover, of the government. This coup was peaceful, and Abboud promised to return Sudan to civilian, or nonmilitary, rule and peaceful elections quickly. Abboud did not keep that promise, however, and resentment toward his rule grew.

Abboud was no more popular in the south, where the civil war raged on. Although the government controlled most of the major towns in the south, the rebels controlled the countryside. Abboud continued to enforce Islamic and Arabic traditions in the south.

By 1964, Abboud's unpopular rule led to widespread riots. In October, he handed power to a civilian prime minister and called for elections. These elections, held in 1965, led to a government coalition between the Umma party and the NUP. These two groups quickly fell into disagreement, however, and for the next four years Sudan had a series of ineffective governments.

A New Ruler

In 1969, the military staged another coup. This one, led by Colonel Jafaar an Nimeiri, abolished parliament and banned all political parties. The leaders of the revolt formed the Revolutionary Command Council and instituted what they called Sudanese socialism. They brought much of Sudan's industry, banking, and businesses under direct government control. Nimeiri became the prime minister.

Politically, Nimeiri faced strong resistance from the Ansar, and Nimeiri's forces fought a battle against the Ansar in 1970. Nimeiri's army won, killing the Ansar's religious leader and sending their political leader, Sadiq al Mahdi (the great grandson of the Mahdi), into exile in Egypt. Sudan's Communists then staged their own coup in 1971, which lasted for three days until Nimeiri's forces restored him to power.

Sudanese soldiers rest following the May 1969 takeover of Khartoum, led by Colonel Jafaar an Nimeiri.

Achieving Peace

With his main northern rivals defeated, Nimeiri turned his attention to the south. He arranged for peaceful talks in Addis Ababa, Ethiopia, where the two sides came to an agreement. Southerners would be granted autonomy, which meant they could rule themselves in everything that did not affect the rest of the nation, and they would be included in the national government and in the army. Arabic was recognized as Sudan's official language, but English would be used in the south's government and schools. Both sides agreed to a cease-fire. The Addis Ababa Accords were signed on March 27, 1972, ending seventeen years of civil war.

Once peace had been established with the south, Nimeiri turned his attention back to the north. He created a people's assembly to write a constitution for Sudan. This constitution was adopted in 1973. It declared that Islam was the nation's official religion, but it also recognized Christianity. Meanwhile, Nimeiri worked to improve relations with the United States and western Europe.

The Ansar, who opposed close ties with the West, wanted Islam to be the only recognized faith in Sudan. In 1976, the Ansar attempted another coup, but they failed. Following this attack, Nimeiri met with Sadiq al Mahdi and agreed to work out a plan that would allow the Ansar influential positions within the government. In 1977, Nimeiri was elected to his second six-year term as president, but major problems still threatened his rule.

CHAPTER TWO

Political Turmoil

Although he had made peace with both the Ansar and the southern rebels, Nimeiri's inability to improve Sudan's economy and accusations of corruption in his government made him unpopular with many Sudanese citizens. In an attempt to regain popularity in the north, in 1983 he divided the southern region into three provinces, which lessened their power in the government. Later that year, influenced by the Umma, he declared that sharia, or strict Islamic law, would be the basis of all law in Sudan. These steps infuriated the south, and after more than a decade of peace between the north and south, the civil war began again.

Life Under Sharia

Nimeiri's moves were not popular with everyone in the north, either. Sharia requires people to live strictly according to the traditional laws of Islam, which place restrictions on people's diet and dress and on the role of women. Under sharia, harsh punishments, including execution, stoning,

Famine in Sudan killed more than 400,000 people in the 1980s. Here, people search for loose grain among a delivery of emergency food in 1985.

and amputation, are given to those who break the laws. Since it applies religious laws to daily and political life, few Islamic nations follow the sharia as their primary law. In Sudan, however, it would apply to all citizens, not only Muslims.

For many Sudanese, Nimeiri had gone too far. The imposition of sharia and the renewal of civil war in the south, combined with severe famine, led to protests and strikes against the government. Even Sadiq al Mahdi criticized Nimeiri and was jailed for his comments. In 1985, a group of military officers overthrew Nimeiri and instituted a transitional military council to run the state, promising a rapid return to democracy.

The state was in terrible shape. Factories and farms were producing less than half of their potential, the country had a huge foreign debt, and the people of Sudan faced high prices from inflation. In 1986, the International Monetary Fund declared Sudan bankrupt. Famine in the south and the west killed more than 400,000 Sudanese, and what money the government had went to fighting the southern rebels.

Return to Civilian Rule

As promised, the transitional council held a national election in April 1986. Sadiq al Mahdi and his Umma party won the election. Like earlier civilian governments, Sadiq al Mahdi struggled to maintain control as other parties joined and left his governing coalition. Very little economic progress was made, and sharia was not lifted. In the south, the civil war continued to rage. The Sudanese People's Liberation Army (SPLA), which had become the main rebel army, demanded the lifting of Islamic law and a new constitutional conference.

Sudanese citizens wait in a refugee camp in Kassala, Sudan, for food distribution during the 1984–1985 famine.

In 1988, representatives of the SPLA and parties that opposed Sadiq al Mahdi agreed on several terms that would lead toward peace. When the government refused to implement those plans, Sudanese military leaders sent a message to Sadiq al Mahdi: either he would make peace with the southern rebels or the military would remove him. In March 1989, Sadiq al Mahdi began direct talks with the SPLA. In Sudan, hope for peace was reborn.

A New Dictator

The hope did not last long. On June 30, 1989, army colonel Omar al-Bashir overthrew Sadiq al Mahdi and instituted the Revolutionary Command Council for National Salvation. He allied himself with the National Islamic Front, led by Hassan al-Turabi, which favored extending

Under the strict dictates of sharia, women in Sudan were forced to wear traditional Arabic dress, including a head covering and veil.

sharia throughout Sudan and the Islamic world. Promising to maintain and expand sharia, Bashir and Turabi strengthened Sudan's connections with other anti-Western Islamic states such as Libya, Iraq, and Iran. In addition, they took food from international sources intended for famine relief in the south and gave it to their own supporters in the north. This caused the United States to halt its relief efforts to Sudan in 1990.

Sudan and the West

In 1990, Iraq invaded its neighbor, Kuwait, and threatened Saudi Arabia. Bashir and Turabi did not approve of Iraq's invasion, but they still saw Iraq as a key ally. When the United States led a UN coalition into Saudi Arabia, Kuwait, and Iraq, Sudan sided with Iraq. They called on the United States and other Western powers to withdraw from the Muslim holy lands of the Middle East. Sudan's relations with the West grew even worse.

One of the main international concerns about Sudan was its support of terrorism. In the 1990s, a number of major world terrorists made their homes in Sudan. Also, Sudan had friendly relations with Iraq, Iran, and Libya, each of which was known to harbor and support terrorists. In 1993, the United States officially added Sudan to its list of nations that sponsor terrorism. That kept the U.S. government and American businesses from having economic relations with Sudan. The same year, both the International Monetary Fund and the World Bank declared that Sudan had failed to repay its debts in a timely fashion, and they imposed sanctions that kept Sudan from receiving more financial support.

The Crisis Worsens

In 1993, Bashir disbanded the Revolutionary Command Council in favor of elected officials. With limited opposition, Bashir was easily elected president; he shared power with Turabi, who became speaker of parliament. Following these elections, the government became even more committed to spreading sharia throughout the land.

Meanwhile, the civil war raged on. Close to 2 million people had died as a result of the conflict by the end of the 1990s, and as many as 4 million had

Since the early 1980s, more than 20,000 children have been orphaned by civil war in Sudan. Here, displaced boys arrive at a refugee camp in 2002.

SUDAN AND INTERNATIONAL TERRORISM

In 1993, the United States added Sudan to its list of State Sponsors of Terrorism. Sudan joined Cuba, Iran, Iraq, Libya, North Korea, and Syria on that list (Iraq was removed from the list in 2004). This put significant restrictions and limitations on Sudan's relationship with the United States and with businesses that work with the United States.

The main accusations against Sudan came from its connections to several internationally recognized terrorist organizations. Iraq's Abu Nidal, Egypt's Islamic Jihad and Jamaat al-Islamiyya, Palestine's Islamic Jihad and Hamas, and Lebanese-based Hezbollah were all active in Sudan in the early 1990s. In addition, Carlos the Jackal, one of the world's most feared terrorists and assassins, was captured in Sudan in 1994. Osama bin Laden, who was responsible for the 2001 terrorist attacks in New York and Washington, D.C., lived in Sudan from 1991 until 1996. His al Qaeda organization operated from bases in Khartoum and other parts of Sudan for those five years.

When Omar al-Bashir and Hassan al-Turabi came to power in 1989, they immediately allied Sudan more closely with anti-Western nations such as Libya, Iran, and Iraq. By supporting Iraq's invasion of Kuwait, they alienated the United States and other Western powers even further. Sudanese leaders also accused the leaders of Saudi Arabia of siding with the United States against its brother nations by inviting U.S. troops into Saudi Arabia to oppose Iraq.

Sudan's relationship with Egypt was even more hostile. In 1995, Sudan was accused of being behind an attempted assassination of Egypt's President Hosni Mubarak. Although Sudan denied involvement, it refused to turn over sus-

Once based in Sudan, al Qaeda mastermind Osama bin Laden is still at large after attacking the United States in 2001.

pects in the case, and the UN placed sanctions on Sudan as a result.

In 1998, al Qaeda bombed U.S. embassies in Kenya and Tanzania. The United States claimed that al Qaeda operatives had trained and prepared for the attacks in Sudan. The United States also identified a factory in Khartoum that they accused of manufacturing a chemical weapon called VX. The United States destroyed the factory with a missile strike, although the factory's owner and the Sudanese government argue that the plant produced only pharmaceutical products.

After the al Qaeda attacks in the United States in 2001, Sudan began to distance itself from terrorism. Bashir had Turabi arrested in 2001; most Western nations believed Turabi was the main connection between Sudan and the terrorist organizations. Bashir also promised to cooperate with the U.S. War on Terror. A State Department terrorism report in 2004 lists several advances made by Sudan, including raids of suspected training camps, counterterrorism agreements with several nations, and the active protection of U.S. interests in Sudan. Continued progress in that field may persuade the United States to remove Sudan from its list of State Sponsors of Terrorism.

fled their homes and become refugees. Many of the deaths were from disease and starvation that resulted from the loss of homes, food and water supplies, and health care as civilians fled the fighting. In order to take away the rebels' home bases, the government attacked villages, killing men, raping women, then burning the homes. For the survivors, slavery and forced labor were common. Many people abandoned their homes before the government forces got there and made their way to the relative safety of refugee camps.

These camps, most of which were in nations that border Sudan, put huge financial and health burdens on those nations. In 1993, the heads of Kenya, Uganda, Eritrea, and Ethiopia met as part of the Intergovernmental Authority on Development (IGAD) to try to work out a peace plan for Sudan, but their efforts were ignored by Sudan's government.

A New Threat

In addition to the ongoing war in the south, regions in the north and the west were becoming increasingly restless. The famines and shortages hit the countryside the hardest, and most of the goods that were available went to the government's supporters. In 1995, a group of parties that opposed Bashir in the north joined the southern rebels in forming the National Democratic Alliance (NDA). This threatened to open a new front in the civil war, forcing the government to divide its forces between the south and the north.

The government moved quickly to address this new threat. After a series of meetings with the northern parties in 1996 and 1997, they announced agreements that gave new government positions to many of the NDA leaders. This freed the government to concentrate again on the southern rebels.

Growing Isolation

As the civil war continued, Sudan's foreign relations were growing worse. In 1995, Egyptian leaders accused the Sudanese government of attempting to assassinate Egyptian president Hosni Mubarak. Although the attempt failed, the accusation led the UN to place further sanctions on Sudan. In addition, because of Sudan's ongoing relationships with recognized terrorists, the United States suspended U.S. embassy operations in 1996 and increased its sanctions on Sudan in 1997.

Sudanese president Omar al-Bashir (left) and Parliament speaker Hassan al-Turabi (right) pose during a military parade in 1995.

In 1999, Sudan's increasing isolation and economic disintegration brought the government to a point of crisis. Parliament attempted to increase the power of its speaker, Turabi, and limit Bashir's influence. Bashir declared a state of emergency, dissolved parliament, suspended the constitution, and named a new cabinet. Turabi was stripped of power.

The New Sudan Police perform a weapons drill in 2005. Many Sudanese are cautiously optimistic that a new peace accord will bring calm to the region.

In December 2000, Bashir held new elections. Many opposition parties boycotted the election, choosing not to participate as a way to protest Bashir's absolute control of the country. As a result, Bashir and his party won the elections easily.

Forced from power, Turabi began to meet with the southern rebels. In 2001, he was arrested for treason after signing an agreement with the rebels that called for peaceful resistance to Bashir. After a period of house arrest, he was moved to a maximum-security prison, where he remained until 2003.

Improving Relations

After Turabi's arrest, Bashir began to show a willingness to work with groups that he had long opposed. After the September 2001 terrorist attacks in the United States, Bashir publicly renounced violence and offered Sudan's cooperation in combating terrorism. This improved diplomatic relations between Sudan and the United States, although Bashir did not approve of the United States taking direct military action: "We are against any attack in Afghanistan or any other countries in which civilians can be the victims,"[3] he told reporters. Turabi's arrest helped Bashir's relations with the West, because Turabi was considered an Islamic extremist with ties to terrorists.

Bashir also opened discussions with the main rebel forces. Outside nations aided the process. The United States appointed a special envoy to help promote the peace talks, some of which were held in Machakos, Kenya. These talks led to an agreement in July 2002 that outlined a basic structure for peace. According to the agreement, southern Sudan would have autonomy for six years, after which they would be allowed to vote on independence from Sudan. This agreement brought about a truce in the civil war.

Peace in the South

After further negotiations, the Sudanese government and the southern rebels signed a formal peace accord in Nairobi, Kenya, in January 2005. The accord included a power-sharing agreement, making rebel leader John Garang a vice president in Bashir's government. The south was made exempt from sharia, and the north and south agreed to share a roughly even split of Sudan's oil revenue. Aid money from outside nations immediately began to pour into southern Sudan as the south prepared to welcome home more than a million refugees. According to the accord, in 2011, southern Sudanese will vote on their independence.

In Sudan, the peace accord was met with cautious optimism. Many events could lead to a renewal of the fighting, but many Sudanese were hopeful that this peace would be a lasting one.

CHAPTER THREE

Sudan's Future

Even as the southern civil war appeared to be coming to an end, a new crisis was worsening in western Sudan. In the region of Darfur, war broke out that was as violent and devastating as the southern civil war had been. Unlike the conflict between the north and the south, in Darfur there is not a significant religious division; most of the estimated 6 million residents of Darfur are Muslims. Instead, the conflict is between the black Africans, who are mostly farmers and remain in one place working their small plots of land, and the Arab herdsmen who migrate in search of water and food for their cattle and camels.

A Crisis Ignored

Darfur lies mostly within the Sahara region. Resources are scarce, and droughts are common. When sanctions caused foreign nations to cut their aid to Sudan, the food and equipment that would normally have reached Darfur disappeared. In large part, the farmers in Darfur controlled the few areas that had access to water and good soil. As drought and famine

Sudanese refugees from the violent civil war in Darfur make their way to a refugee camp in Chad in 2004.

A Sudanese woman carries water on her head in a refugee camp for persons displaced by civil war in Darfur.

began to spread, the herders brought their animals to these fertile areas. Through the 1980s and 1990s, small battles between the herders and farmers were common as the farmers tried to protect their crops from the nomadic herds.

When the government and the southern rebels began to move toward peace in 2002, many in Darfur wanted their region to be a part of the peace plans. Darfur's farmers wanted protection from the herdsmen, and they hoped that the peace process would include peace for all of Sudan.

Neither the southern rebels nor Bashir's government showed interest in including Darfur in the peace process, however. To the government, Darfur was less of a threat than the ongoing war in the south, and the southerners were not willing to add anyone else's cause to their own.

The New Rebellion

When it became apparent that Darfur was not to be a part of the peace process, many of the farmers in Darfur came together in protest. In early 2003, two rebel organizations appeared: the Sudan Liberation Movement/Army (SLM/A) and the Justice for Equality Movement (JEM). The SLM/A was created, in part ,out of other groups that had long opposed the government, and JEM was made up primarily of supporters of

In response to the uprising of government opposition groups, janjaweed militiamen set the village of Chero Kasi ablaze in September 2004.

A woman surveys the damage done to a house by a bomb dropped in the northern Darfur town of Tawilah.

the former speaker of parliament, Hassan al-Turabi. The two groups had few ideas in common other than their opposition to Bashir's government, but they were able to work together.

In April 2003, SLM/A soldiers attacked government forces at El Fasher in northern Darfur. Soon after, African farms and villages began to be attacked by roving bands of Arab horsemen called janjaweed. These attacks usually included acts of murder, torture, and rape against the villagers. One survivor described an attack: "They came at 4 A.M. on horse-back, on camels, in vehicles, with two helicopters overhead. . . . They killed 50 people in my village. My father, grandmother, uncle and two brothers were all killed. . . . They don't want any blacks left."[4] Both the SLM/A and JEM have also been accused of equally violent attacks against those who oppose them, though those reports are less frequent.

Crimes Against Humanity

The SLM/A and JEM accused the government of arming and support-ing the janjaweed. The government denied this claim, but the UN found evidence to support it. In a report to the UN Security Council in February 2005, UN secretary-general Kofi Annan stated: "A pattern arose of a com-bination of military and militia forces (janjaweed) attacking rebel positions and burning villages. The attack on Hamada village on 13 January 2005 represented a particularly severe case, with large numbers of women and children killed." The same report described "large-scale killings of civilians in villages in Southern Darfur, accompanied by reports of abduction and rape."[5]

The treatment of women in Darfur is of particular concern to many world aid organizations and outside observers. A UN human rights expert, Yakin Ertürk, visited Darfur in 2004 and reported:

> Women and girls have suffered multiple forms of violence during attacks on their villages, including rape, killings, the burning of homes and pillage of livestock. Women have also been tortured during interrogation by security forces for being

WOMEN IN SUDAN

One major area of international concern in Sudan is the treatment of women. Women have been the primary victims of violence in both the southern civil war and in Darfur. Even outside of the war zones, however, women have been subject to mistreatment and discrimination. Some of this comes from cultural traditions, and some of it is tied to religious beliefs.

In the north especially, there are a number of laws designed to limit opportunities for women. In 2000, the governor of Khartoum passed a law that banned women from working in public places. Although that law was eventually blocked in court, similar restrictions remained in place throughout the north. Although some women have found more opportunities in the cities in recent years, the enforcement of sharia law limits women's legal rights and the public role they can play.

Women may not be religious scholars or clergy; they may not hold any prominent jobs, including significant government positions; and they must dress modestly or face severe punishments.

In the south, too, women's opportunities are limited by tradition. According to a March 2005 article in the *Los Angeles Times*, "1% of women in southern Sudan finish primary school and 88% are illiterate." The expectation for women is that they will marry— usually while they are teenagers. Women are seen as valuable property and a source of wealth. For example, a man might give property, such as cows, to a potential bride's family when he wants to marry their daughter. It is also acceptable for a man to have more than one wife, although a woman who commits adultery could be subject to jail, beatings, or death.

Women's health care is also a problem throughout the nation.

Female genital mutilation is common in Sudan, and reproductive health care is poor. In 2003, the World Health Organization stated that between only 6 and 12 percent of births took place in health care facilities, and maternity mortality (death during childbirth) was among the highest in the world.

The worst treatment of women, however, has been in Sudan's war zones. Throughout both periods of the civil war and in the conflict in Darfur, women have been frequent targets of rape. This has been used to force them to abandon their homes and villages. At times rape has been used for racial impact: Janjaweed attackers have been accused of trying to produce lighter-skinned babies by raping black African women. Even in the refugee camps, women are afraid to leave guarded and protected areas for fear of attack.

Health care for women in Sudan in sparse. Here, a Sudanese refugee and her child await health care from a humanitarian organization in Chad.

relatives of suspected rebels. I heard numerous accounts of continuing violence against the displaced women and girls allegedly by government-backed militia and security forces.[6]

The ongoing crimes brought increased world attention. In 2004, U.S. secretary of state Colin Powell declared that he found evidence of genocide in Darfur, which meant that the black Africans were being intentionally wiped out as a group. His finding was disputed by a UN investigation in early 2005, which stated that the UN did not find evidence of genocide, but that the finding should not "detract from the gravity of the crimes perpetrated . . . (which may be) no less serious and heinous than genocide."[7]

Sudan's Many Challenges

Despite several attempted truces and cease-fires in Darfur, the fighting continued from 2003 through early 2005. By February 2005, the UN estimated that 2.5 million people had been directly affected by the fighting in Darfur, including victims of violence and those displaced from their homes. The UN also predicted further drought and famine if the violence was not halted so that aid could be delivered.

Even outside of the bloodshed in Darfur, Sudan faces many significant challenges. Although there was hope in 2005 that the southern civil war had finally ended, the south is left with a lost generation. These are the young adults in the south who grew up during the civil war without access to education or job training. They have minimal health care, few resources, and no experience in government or management. Some people are skeptical of the prospect of eventual independence for the south. They

A Sudanese Liberation Movement/Army member guards Ashma Village in south Darfur.

question whether Sudan's leaders will really give up the arable land and oil reserves in the south.

Bashir's willingness to end the war in the south helped him repair some of Sudan's relationships with western Europe and the United States, but internally there are many threats to his power. His former rival, Turabi, was released from prison in 2003 but jailed again in 2004 for aiding the Darfur rebels. Turabi remains popular with many of the more extreme Islamic elements in Sudan, who in turn are supported by extremists in other nations. On the other hand, those who support democracy in Sudan also oppose Bashir and his fixed elections.

Crises affecting its neighbors also pose challenges to Sudan's stability. In recent years, revolutions and uprisings in Uganda and Congo have spilled over the borders into Sudan, bringing in refugees and armed troops that add to Sudan's own troubles. Other unstable neighbors, such as Chad, Ethiopia, and Eritrea, have been of concern, and Sudan's own refugees from the civil war and Darfur have added to the health and political woes in those nations.

Sudan's Hope

The one area that appears brightest for Sudan is its oil. The end of the southern civil war opened opportunities for the increased development of Sudan's oil production. Foreign nations and oil companies who were reluctant to work in Sudan during the war began negotiating with Sudan as the civil war came to an end. At the end of 2004, several business reports claimed that Sudan's oil output could double within a year. That would mean a great deal more money for Sudan's government; if used properly,

Women refugees fleeing violence in Darfur head toward the village of Shigekaro in search of food aid. Scenes such as this one remain common in Sudan.

it could be put toward programs to combat drought and famine. On the other hand, if the money goes only to the government leaders, it would only increase the economic imbalance in Sudan, leading to further unrest.

Sudan's future depends upon its ability to establish peace in Darfur and maintain peace in the south. Sudan's divided population and its challenges of drought, famine, and geography are so severe that only through cooperation and peace will the nation ever be able to thrive. It will also almost certainly need to build stronger international partnerships to develop its resources and insure against future drought and famine; some question whether that will ever happen under Bashir's leadership. Until Sudan commits itself to stopping the bloodshed in the west, however, its hope for a successful future is limited.

Important Dates

750 B.C.	The armies of Cush conquer Egypt; the Cushite king Piye founds Egypt's Twenty-fifth Dynasty.
300 B.C.	Height of Meroë society
A.D. **6th century**	Christian missionaries begin spreading Christianity in Sudan
7th century	Muslim armies spread Islam into northern Africa
1821	Egypt conquers northern Sudan
1823	Egypt establishes Khartoum as Sudan's capital
1881	Revolt led by the Mahdi against British and Egyptians
1898	A British-Egyptian force defeats Mahdists at Battle of Omdurman
1924	British force out Egyptians and take sole control of Sudan
1946	Britain announces that southern Sudan and northern Sudan will be joined
1955	Civil war begins in southern Sudan
1956	Sudan becomes independent
1969	Military coup led by Jafaar an Nimeiri
1972	Addis Ababa Accords signed, ending seventeen years of civil war
1983	Nimeiri declares sharia, or strict Islamic law, over all of Sudan; civil war begins again
1985	Nimeiri overthrown
1986	Sadiq al Mahdi and his Umma party win national election
1989	Omar al-Bashir takes over government, ending peace talks with rebels
1993	United States adds Sudan to list of nations that support terror; International Monetary Fund and World Bank impose sanctions that keep financial support from Sudan
1996–1998	United States suspends embassy operations in Sudan, increases economic sanctions, and bombs alleged chemical weapons plant in Khartoum
2001	Hassan al-Turabi arrested; Bashir promises support against terrorism
2002	North and south reach basic agreement for peace
2003	Major conflict begins in Darfur
2004	U.S. secretary of state Colin Powell travels to Darfur and declares findings of genocide
2005	Formal peace accord signed between north and south; UN does not find evidence of genocide in Darfur but determines that 2.5 million people had been directly affected by the fighting in Darfur

For More Information

BOOKS

Daniel E. Harmon, *Sudan: 1880 to the Present.* Philadelphia: Chelsea House, 2001.

Patricia Levy, *Sudan.* New York: Marshall Cavendish, 1997.

Salome C. Nnoromele, *Sudan.* San Diego: Lucent, 2004.

Gail Snyder, *Sudan.* Philadelphia: Mason Crest, 2003.

Judy Walgren, *The Lost Boys of Natinga: A School for Southern Sudan's Young Refugees.* Boston: Houghton Mifflin, 1998.

Lawrence J. Zwier, *Sudan: North Against South.* Minneapolis: Lerner, 1999.

WEB SITES

Darfur: A Genocide We Can Stop (www.darfurgenocide.org). An antigovernment site devoted to stopping genocide in Darfur.

Embassy of the Republic of Sudan (www.sudanembassy.org). The Web site of the Sudanese embassy in the United States.

Governments on the WWW: Sudan (www.gksoft.com/govt/en/sd.html). Links to official Sudanese government Web pages.

Human Rights Watch (www.hrw.org/doc?t=africa&c=sudan). The Human Rights Watch page on Sudan.

Sudan Net (www.sudan.net). Huge amounts of information and resources on Sudan, including history, government, and culture.

SU LAIR: Africa South of the Sahara (www-sul.stanford.edu/depts/ssrg/africa/sudan.html). Stanford University's links to Sudan information.

U.S. Department of State (www.state.gov/r/pa/ei/bgn/5424.htm). U.S. State Department page on Sudan.

WHO in Sudan (www.emro.who.int/sudan). The World Health Organization page on Sudan.

Source Quotations

1. Quoted in "U.S. Calls Killings in Sudan Genocide," *Washington Post*, September 10, 2004.

2. Article 17, United Nations International Law Commission. www.un.org/law/ilc/texts/dcode.htm.

3. Quoted in "Sudan to Target Terrorists," *Houston Chronicle*, September 19, 2001.

4. Quoted in Darfur: A Genocide We Can Stop. www.darfurgenocide.org.

5. Quoted in United Nations Security Council, "Report of the Secretary General on the Sudan," February 4, 2005, pp. 3–4.

6. Quoted in United Nations High Commissioner for Human Rights, "UN Women's Rights Expert Concludes Visit to Sudan," October 6, 2004, p. 1.

7. "UN Finds No Evidence of Genocide in Darfur", *Washington Post*, February 1, 2005.

Index

47

About the Author

Chris Hughes holds a B.A. in history from Lafayette College and an M.A. in social studies education from Lehigh University. A history teacher and school administrator, Hughes teaches both U.S. and world history and has written several books on the American Civil War and on developing nations. Hughes currently lives and works at a boarding school in Chatham, Virginia, with his wife, Farida, and their children, Jordan and Leah.